To Daniella
Here's to your
sucess & Prosperity
:) Carol Doherty

MW00592546

KEEP IT!

The Small Business Owners Guide to Keeping
More Of Your Hard-Earned Money

Copyright © 2018 CelebrityPress® LLC

All rights reserved. No part of this book may be used or reproduced in any manner whatsoever without prior written consent of the author, except as provided by the United States of America copyright law.

Published by CelebrityPress®, Orlando, FL.

CelebrityPress® is a registered trademark.

Printed in the United States of America.

ISBN: 978-1-7322843-8-8
LCCN: 2018961125

This publication is designed to provide accurate and authoritative information with regard to the subject matter covered. It is sold with the understanding that the publisher is not engaged in rendering legal, accounting, or other professional advice. If legal advice or other expert assistance is required, the services of a competent professional should be sought. The opinions expressed by the authors in this book are not endorsed by CelebrityPress® and are the sole responsibility of the author rendering the opinion.

Most CelebrityPress® titles are available at special quantity discounts for bulk purchases for sales promotions, premiums, fundraising, and educational use. Special versions or book excerpts can also be created to fit specific needs.

For more information, please write:
CelebrityPress®
520 N. Orlando Ave, #2
Winter Park, FL 32789
or call 1.877.261.4930

Visit us online at: www.CelebrityPressPublishing.com

KEEP IT!

The Small Business Owners Guide to Keeping
More Of Your Hard-Earned Money

CelebrityPress®
Winter Park, Florida

CONTENTS

FOREWORD

<u>An important FORWARD to this book. Read First.</u>

My name is Chauncey Forward Hutter, Jr.

Yes, my middle name is "Forward", and this is the first time I've ever written a foreword for a book. So, read it … I promise to make it worth your time!

--oo---ooo---OOO---ooo---oo--

It was Friday night, March 31st, my mom's 77th birthday. We had just finished blowing out the candles at my parent's house when the phone call came.

"Why are you not in the hospital … did you see the test results?" my cardio doctor asked with a frustrated tone.

I said, "No, the stress test nurses sent me home."

"Well, your heart has blockages in five different areas … I'm in the process of finding you a bed in the hospital right now."

"Tonight?" I asked. "How about after the weekend? I could check myself in on Monday once my wife returns from her out-of-town trip."

"Did you notice your blood pressure dropped 65 points after three minutes on a treadmill? Didn't you feel extremely dizzy … I'm shocked you didn't pass out!" the doctor exclaimed. "Sorry Mr. Hutter, but staying home this weekend is too risky. We must get you to a place where we can monitor your heart 24/7."

My brother-in-law drove me a short distance to the University of Virginia hospital and dropped me off before visiting hours were over that night. The only problem was, I was not visiting. I spent the next 15 days in this hospital "hotel" that felt like a prison.

Now, don't get me wrong.

I'm EXTREMELY thankful a persistent nurse practitioner would not take "No" for an answer, and kindly but sternly encouraged me NOT to leave town to be a chaperon on my daughter's high school trip a couple days earlier. I finally agreed to take the stress test sooner rather than later and thank God I did.

I was a heart attack just waiting to happen. But instead, no major episode happened. Severe damage to my body or mind averted.

Failing the stress test was the best thing that could have happened to me. Because a couple of days later, the doctors went in and got a closer look at my arteries and determined very quickly I needed heart surgery.

TRIPLE BYPASS HEART SURGERY SAVES MY LIFE

After several baseline tests to determine the best strategy for moving forward, the expert heart surgeons did what they are trained to do. They took my heart out of my body, added three bypasses, put my ticker back in its place and started it back up again.

True transformation.

The lead surgeon told me the next day, everything went great … "you're good for another 40 years now."

"Now let the healing process begin. In several months, you'll feel better than ever!"

So, here's the lesson I want you to get …

I was walking around doing life and did not realize the seriousness of the hour I was living in.

Yes, I did feel some symptoms. I couldn't breathe as well as I used to. But when I showed up to my regular cardio check-ups, I always told the doctors I wasn't feeling any pain in my chest. (Because I wasn't.) My symptoms were a little different than normal. Personally, I knew something was not quite right. But I never would have guessed my arteries were over 80% blocked in five separate locations in my heart. The nurse said I was "one-walk-to-the-mailbox" from dying.

Not the best picture to imagine, but let's compare my near-death experience to your current situation in your small business.

YOUR TAXES ARE EATING AWAY AT THE MONEY YOU ARE SUPPOSED TO KEEP!

Most small business owners will deny this fact. They think they are paying Uncle Sam what everybody else has to pay and they can't do anything about it.

However, when I speak with small business owners face-to-face, they'll admit there are financial red-flags in their bookkeeping, payroll and tax reporting. Storm clouds (symptoms) have drifted over their operation and are now in sight of their core business activities.

No business owner wants their company to bleed-to-death

because of cash-flow issues or tax problems. The question is, "Will you reach out for help before your financial symptoms get worse?"

"WHO'S THIS GUY NAMED ... FICA?"

My first introduction to taxes was when I was sixteen years old and I was working as a lifeguard at the pool where our family went in the summer. I think I was probably making three dollars an hour. I worked twenty hours that first week, so I was looking forward to getting my first paycheck. I could do the math: twenty hours times three bucks. I was going to get paid sixty dollars. The paycheck came, and I opened up the envelope to see my sixty-dollar check. It was only for fifty-two dollars? I thought, "What happened here? Somebody took my money!"

I went home to my dad, and I showed him the check, and I said, "Dad! Who's FICA? FICA's got some of this money!" He laughed SO hard. My dad said, "Hold on a second." And he called in my mom from the kitchen, still laughing, "Honey, honey, come here. Okay, Chauncey say that again. Ask me that same question again ... listen to this."

And I said, "Well, I just wanted to know who FICA is. He has some of my money. Just look at my paycheck." And they both busted out in laughter. Then my dad proclaimed, "Welcome to the real world, son. It's called death and taxes." Then he proceeded to give me that whole speech ... and that was my first introduction to Uncle Sam.

My dad was a tax professional for 50 years before he retired. He lived a life helping regular people KEEP the IRS off their back and so his clients could KEEP the most money legally possible in their pocket.

The same is true for the professional tax and accounting practitioners in this book, *Keep It*.

They have dedicated their lives to helping small business owners be more successful by SHOWING YOU HOW TO KEEP AS MUCH OF YOUR HARD-EARNED MONEY IN YOUR BANK ACCOUNT AS LEGALLY POSSIBLE!

If you are a small business owner reading this book, you are in the right place.

As a wise old (rich) man once said, "It's not how much money you make … it's how much you keep."

This book provides MANY different ways to save money on your taxes and techniques for reducing the extra expenses in your business. Either way, you KEEP more of your money. And that's the place where your money is supposed to be – with you!

Lastly, it's an excellent time of life to own and operate a small business. Increased wealth is waiting for you right around the corner. My advice is … **Go For It!**

And I look *forward* to hearing about your tax-saving success gleaned from the pages inside this book.

Enjoy!

Chauncey FORWARD Hutter, Jr

- www.taxmarketing.com

CHAPTER 1

TAX SAVINGS FROM THE SUPER-RICH

BY RICHARD COLOMBIK, ESQ., CPA

Hey, you want to save income taxes? … on Federal and State, correct?

Do you own your own business? Well, if you do, you are halfway there to tax savings and *Keeping it!*

Federal income taxation is based upon a concept of taxable income. Any legal manner you can reduce your business and your personal taxable income for the current year, results in reduced income taxation. If you reduce your taxable income sufficiently, then you also may reduce your income tax bracket which also reduces your income tax! (Your income tax bracket is the rate at which your income is taxed.) Business owners have a broader range of income tax deductions than individuals, so it is easier to reduce a business owner's taxable income.

Okay, easy concept, right? Now, let's build upon that.

First, there are only two broad categories to reduce income taxation. When you reduce income taxation it is either (a) **FOREVER**, called a permanent difference, such as municipal bond interest never being includible federally as taxable income, or (b) **A CHANGE**, which may be a timing difference—such as a 401(k) account, where you do not pay income tax today, but will pay income tax in the future. A timing difference does not change the character of the funds from being taxed, but the timing of when such funds will be taxed. This is referred to as a timing difference.

A subcategory may be referred to as a combination of the two broad categories, where you obtain a timing difference today, and do not pay taxes today. But in the future, the funds are taxed at a lower tax rate or in a classification of income which is taxed at a rate less than ordinary income, such as a qualified dividend or a long-term capital gain. For example, today the maximum capital gain rate and the maximum rate on qualified dividends is 20%, whereas the maximum rate on ordinary income is taxed at 37%. Therefore, if you could combine a timing difference to defer when your income is taxed, combined with being taxed at a lower rate, you would have a permanent difference between the tax rates, in this example, 37% less 20% = 17% savings, plus you would defer your taxation into a future period. A deferral of taxation allows you to invest the income tax funds and have them available, plus profits or gains when your income tax is due. Some techniques that are approved by the IRS may defer your taxation for 30 years! That is a long time, where you can grow your assets substantially.

Now that we have these basic concepts on the table, what do we do with them and how can the owner of a closely-held business apply them?

Let's introduce a few concepts to help you understand how this might apply to most businesses. I say most businesses, because there are technical differences between business structures, and a thorough analysis of each income tax and financial situation is required for precise and proper application. Let's look at a simple permanent difference that almost all businesses, except a

Schedule C entity, that a taxpayer may use.

Ready? Can it really be that easy? Yes!

You own a business. You also own a residence where you or you and your family reside. During the year you meet with clients, you entertain clients, you meet with people that work for you, as well as your financial, tax, legal professionals and others. You even have an office party once a year. Your residence is 2,000 square feet. To help with your tax planning and to make your setting a bit less formal you decide to have annually 12 meetings including an office party at your home. You have valid reasons for the meetings, as you could have rented a hotel room or other facility for privacy or to be more comfortable out of the office.

You check the prices of renting a high-level hotel suite that is 2,000 square feet and find out the price is $4,500 per night, $2.25 per sq. foot. You most assuredly as a prudent business person do not want to spend that much. You do want to have privacy and a more comfortable atmosphere. You even check with most high-quality hotels in the area and find out that even a smaller hotel rents a 300 sq. foot hotel room for $300 per night or $1 per square foot.

Wait, why not have the meetings at your home? Your home is comfortable, you can get a better relationship with your professionals, some clients, your staff. H-m-m… great idea! You also decide to have your company reimburse you for $1 per foot, for $2,000 sq. feet for 12 valid meetings for the year. (Note: you could use it 14 days per year, but we will be conservative.) So, for the year, your business pays you $2,000 per meeting for 12 meetings or $24,000. Big deal, right? Wrong. Real big deal! The business can now deduct the $24,000 as a rental expense, and you do NOT have to pay income tax on the funds received! This is a permanent difference as you will never pay income tax on these funds? Why?

That is the IRS rule for *de minimis* rental income on real estate. See IRC Sec. 280A. You may rent property for 14 days per calendar year and do not have to report such income on your income tax return.

H-m-m... I just saved $24,000 x 37% (income tax bracket) or $8,880. Good start, and you paid for the book too! The book should also be deductible as an expense for your business to do tax planning. Again, talk to your tax professional. The home rental is technically not a tax-free fringe benefit, so business ownership rules do not apply to limit who can receive this benefit, as opposed to tax-free fringe benefits which do have limitations for business owners. Schedule C owners still cannot have this benefit. By the way, I do not recommend being a Schedule C for a business due to many income tax and asset protection issues.

Another usage of permanent differences addresses the usage of tax-free fringe benefits. This area gets a bit more complex as a tax-free fringe benefit is a program designed to cover all employees, which is deductible by the company but not taxable to the employee. This does not apply to all business structures if the owner wants to receive a benefit, as in many passthrough entities the owner is not considered an employee, even if on the payroll! Very common in S Corporations, as a 2% or more owner is not deemed an employee for fringe benefit purposes. Well, how will that help me?

There are two areas to consider. Does your business pay outside companies to perform separate and distinct business operations for your company which are costly? An example would be a company hiring an outside firm to do a marketing and promotion campaign. If a new firm was formed that you did not directly own, which performed the marketing tasks at a fair market, arm's length rate and you were an employee of it, then you would qualify for tax-free fringe benefits from this new entity. Tax-free fringe benefits may be significant, depending again upon your business structure, but between $20,000 to $100,000 per year of tax-deductible payments to you from this new entity may be possible. If you were in a 37% income tax bracket, this could result in significant permanent tax savings. 37% of $100,000 is $37,000 plus state income tax savings. Now this technique will not work with all businesses and with all functions, but with proper review and analysis it may work for you and your company!

What else have you not heard about that can help your business and save you money?

If sufficient risk is present, then the formation of a captive insurance company where you are one of a group of owners may be attractive. Captives are currently a popular business planning and risk management tool. Their true benefit is risk management, but they also have income tax benefits as well. Some companies aggregate business owners so that smaller amount of risk would be possible to cover and still make a captive insurance company viable. When I say smaller, potentially $100,000 of insurable risk would be deemed "smaller" for a captive's purposes.

Let's talk about captive insurance for a few moments. A captive insurance company is a valid and licensed property and casualty insurance company formed in any state that allows for such a company, and commonly elects under IRC Sec. 831(b) not to pay income tax on premiums received. This allows the company to potentially be more profitable that an insurance company that pays income tax on premium income. A small company that has this valid election pays income tax only on taxable investment income, hence a very small amount of income tax would be paid by such a company. Presuming the company is a valid insurance company, and you own all or a portion of it, then the premiums paid are deductible by your business within IRC Sec. 162, but the receipt of such income by your insurance company is not subject to income taxation. Small for purposes of this IRC section is $2,300,000 per annum! Small, right? . . . lol!

There are some high-quality, captive management firms that

provide captives as a turnkey solution where they form, manage, hire professionals to handle operations and claims management. They also combine multiple businesses into a single captive to reduce costs of formation and operation.

If this may be a good fit, you obtain insurance coverage from a company of which you are an owner. The premiums received are not subject to income tax. You have deducted those premium payments but now you want to terminate your ownership.

You are now "coming out" of the insurance company, which has multiple owners. As your company has been profitable, your stock is now worth more money than you initially invested. The company buys back your stock (technically a redemption) and you pay a capital gains tax on your gain. Big deal? Well, your business received an ordinary deduction for premiums paid and now your gain is taxed as a long-term capital gain. The deduction was at your ordinary income tax rate, 37%, and your gain is taxed as a capital gain, maximum tax rate of 20%. Hence, you have deferred your income tax on your insurance profits, a timing difference, and, when you receive your profits via a stock sale, you have taxation at a lower income tax rate, a permanent difference. This is a combination of the two major tax savings concepts and a very powerful tool.

Let's look at a more interesting concept that is not widely used. If you have already sold your business and retired, are you living off your retirement income? Interest, dividends, capital gains? Do you like a year-round sunny climate, beaches, golf courses, and a slower pace of life? Would you like to reduce your income tax rate from 37% to 0%? 0%? Legal? YES!

What do you have to do?

Move to beautiful Puerto Rico and register under the Puerto Rican Act 22, tax grant. This Act allows Puerto Rican residents to exclude specific types of interest, dividends and capital gains from income taxation – no federal tax, no state tax, no tax! As Puerto Rico is a US Possession, there is no passport required, you do not lose your citizenship as Puerto Rico residents are US citizens, and the Internal Revenue Code has specific provisions that bona fide Puerto Rico residents only pay income tax in Puerto Rico!

Puerto Rico has had income tax incentives since after World War II, beginning in approximately in 1947. Their business tax act, currently Act 20, grants certain businesses that do business exclusively outside of Puerto Rico, e.g., within the United States, an income tax rate of only 4%! That is right, 4%. Plus, the dividends that are paid to the company owner are exempt from Puerto Rico taxation. WOW!

So, the big sacrifice is to live in Paradise. Could be worse.

Business owners are the big winners. Income tax deductions, ways to reduce taxation, tax-free money, fringe benefits, also ask your tax preparer about the new qualified business income deduction. Tax rates are currently low, but with proper and sustained planning they can be substantially lower.

About Richard

Richard M. Colombik, Esq., CPA is an award-winning Attorney and CPA with a Doctorate in Jurisprudence with Distinction, who was formerly on the tax staff of one of the world's wealthiest families. Mr. Colombik has also been a tax manager at a Big Four accounting firm, the State Bar's liaison to the Internal Revenue Service, Vice President of the American Association of Attorney-CPAs, Vice Chairman of the American Bar Association's Tax Section of the General Practice Council, Past Chair of the Illinois State Bar Association's Federal Tax Committee. Mr. Colombik was on the liaison committee to the IRS, including a stint with the Washington National office, a member of the Asset Protection Committee, ABA, and the Captive Insurance subcommittee, ABA. He was featured in an article from the National Law Journal and referred to as one of the nation's top tax lawyers! He is also been named a Lawyer of Distinction ranking within the top 10% of all attorneys within his state.

Mr. Colombik is a highly sought-after speaker and lecturer and he has appeared on numerous television shows, hosted a weekly radio show on tax and business planning, and has authored numerous articles on income taxation, asset protection planning, IRS defense and estate planning and the impact of Puerto Rico taxation for a U.S. business. This is in addition to authoring a published work on Business Entity Structures offered by the Illinois Institute of Continuing Legal Education. He has also been a featured speaker to business groups, civic groups, bar associations and professional groups. Mr. Colombik has been interviewed and featured in articles by INC Magazine regarding income tax planning, by American Express Online Magazine regarding business changes and how to use them in times of economic uncertainty, and Captive Review regarding Captive Insurance Companies and case commentaries.

He has delivered over 100 lectures and published over 100 articles on taxation and planning. Mr. Colombik's law firm, Richard M. Colombik & Associates, P.C. concentrates in Strategic Tax Planning, Asset Protection, Business Entity Structuring and Transaction, Complex Estate Plans, IRS Defense and Business Planning.

Mr. Colombik is also one of the Managing Members of Tax Law Solutions,

LLC, which is headquartered in San Juan, Puerto Rico, offering creative and proprietary income tax solutions to the affluent closely-held business owner and utilization of Puerto Rico tax grants to assist Puerto Rico and the U.S. taxpayer.

Creative, innovative and strategic planning is Mr. Colombik's forte, concentrating in profitable closely-held business entities.

Contact information for Richard M. Colombik, JD, CPA:
- Illinois office 630-250-5700
- Puerto Rican office 787-200-3359
- www.richardcolombik.com
- taxlawsolutions.net

CHAPTER 2

ELEVEN WAYS TO PROTECT YOUR ACCOUNTING HEALTH

BY LINDA TRENT, CPA

I started my accounting practice thirty years ago and it all began with one client. My first client was an excellent and well-respected farmer in the town I call home. In a community of less than two thousand, we have a tight network of people that all help each other out. If my neighbor needed a ditch dug out, I could refer her to the excavator guy in town. When I need a light post rewired or my sprinklers adjusted I have an electrician and irrigation expert on speed dial. The most valuable lesson I've learned over my years of practicing accounting is that people can truly master their industry, making it always worth the call for their work. While we are all experts in our own professions, we can't do everything ourselves.

I know my passion is accounting, collecting information from a business and putting it together in a way that means something. I have a thirst for solving accounting problems and understanding what numbers mean about the health of a business. I feel accomplished at the end of a client consultation after translating a hefty, intricate tax code into usable, sensible language for a business owner. That being said, I recognized long ago that business owners need to dedicate their time more wisely when it comes to "keeping house" in their business. I almost called it quits when I could not figure out how to network my computers to each other, so I hired a professional.

You can't do everything. Think of it this way: if you earn your living building commercial spaces, you get paid thousands of dollars for each job so why would you spend hours on end trying to create your own balance sheet? Have you seen a client's attempt at doing a job themselves? If it drives you crazy to witness people's misperceptions about your industry, then you know how I feel. If the work we do is easy enough for the inexperienced to tackle, there would be no work for us! Your time is precious, you don't make any money running around in circles trying to micromanage your business all on your own.

I'm here to tell you there are a handful of best practices each of us can implement to take an active role in our accounting health.

1. **Follow your Heart:**
   This is such an overused cliché, but in my years as a tax and accounting professional, I have seen business owners start up and fail time and time again. A handful of those business closures were due to the owner losing interest or discovering hardships in an industry they assumed to be easily profitable. First and foremost, find what you love to do. How could you take a true introspective look if you do not already have a clear vision for yourself and your business? Find something you enjoy doing so much you would do it every day for free, then take that job and figure out how to get paid for it! Be excited to head to the office/jobsite/shop every single day, for without passion for the industry it will be near impossible to think and act critically about your work.

2. **Listen to the Numbers:**
   You should regularly and consistently look at your production, profitability and liquidity as well as income and expenses. These factors speak volumes about the fitness of your business. Minding these will allow you to review/

adapt/ enhance many facets of your establishment. Begin a Monday commitment to quickly review last week and year-to-date figures. There are plenty of software programs out there that can help you track these numbers as you go. Allow yourself time to get to know your business functions on a factual, all-encompassing level.

3. **Collect the Receipt:**
   If you never take a receipt for purchases or crumple them up in the cup holder of your car, STOP. If you are keeping a shoe box of receipts and invoices, STOP. Don't keep your receipts in a big pile to deal with later on. Your receipts should be very important to you, if you don't want to keep them, scan them into a computer and throw the originals away. I can't tell you how many deductions clients have missed out on because they couldn't prove an expense. There is way too much information passing through you for you to be wasting time with receipts in a mess.

4. **Hire a Professional:**
   You aren't using an accountant. Are you kidding? You are the best at what you do (building houses, running a retail store, laying concrete, etc.), but you can't be a professional in everything. If you understand the State and Federal tax codes without schooling and continued education you might be in the wrong industry! You need to get a certified public accountant on your side helping you to understand your situation. There are tax benefits are out there that you might be missing out on. You are an expert in your field, why wouldn't you hire an expert accountant in their field? Apply this to any aspect of your business that you waste your precious time on. Know your weaknesses, if you are a work horse but can't get new clients, hire a third-party marketing group. If money is disappearing left and right, bring in an auditor to look the business over top to bottom.

5. **Build Relationships:**
   Keeping a network of people is invaluable. I pride myself in being a one stop shop for my clients. If you can't provide a service, find a company that will and partner up with them.

For example, my clients can meet with an attorney, financial advisor or business lender in my conference room. It takes one phone call and those professionals will gladly travel to my office to meet with a new client I've referred. If you use a CPA for advice or as a tax preparer, start to keep them aware of the major events in your life. If you get married, divorced, have children, adopt children, children going to college or gain an inheritance, these are major events to tell your CPA about. Each event has pros and cons regarding your tax liabilities. Did you know that you can claim your college children even if they don't live with you? Some of the things you inherit are tax free while other things you inherit could have a tax obligation attached to them.

6. **Have a Type:**
   Make sure to have a proactive accountant in the field of business you are in. If you are a farmer, you don't want to have an accountant in a large city that knows nothing about your business, they won't understand you or be able to help you much. Picking the right accountant doesn't mean they have to be your neighbor. In the world now, your accountant can be anywhere. Technology enables us to connect to specialists across the country. Your accountant should be a "partner" in your business. They should be helping you reach your goals or at least be a sounding board for decisions. You are trying to run your business the best that you can, usually by yourself, why wouldn't you use your best "numbers" person to help you evaluate your condition and give you advice on ideas that you have to make your business better. They may have already had some experience and would be able to help you mull over the idea to see if it really has merit! It's all about dealing with the necessary professional that can help your business become more successful.

7. **Pick up the Phone:**
   Pursue and use the advice or knowledge of the experts. Make the most of your time. Take advantage of an accountant's vast knowledge and experience! Call them up before you buy equipment or sell an asset. Stop by their office after a

record-breaking quarter, most accountants really care about their clients. So much happens in your business life over a year that you need to keep your accountant in the loop. Do you need to incorporate? Is it time to start investing in a retirement account? Can you bring in a partner? Those are just a few things you might consider during the business year.

8. **Invest in a Bookkeeper:**
   If you are running your business effectively, you will make money working for clients rather than for yourself. Spending your time to enter then reconcile your bank statement, pay your bills or chase down accounts receivable will hurt your bottom line in the long run. You MUST review the numbers, maybe even sign the checks, but you don't have to put the check in the envelope and mail it...do you? Do not spend your valuable time to enter huge amounts of data on the computer. The necessary part of this number tracking is the end result. You need to know where you stand, but you do not have to be the one to enter it all.

9. **Think 365:**
   One of the worst oversights I observe small business owners make is that they don't year-end plan. You need to year-end plan because you need to know where you stand. Year-end planning allows you to see if you have made way too much money or if you need to end up with a loss. What status are your assets and liabilities in? There are a lot of things you can do to better your tax situation, but you have to do most of them before December 31st. If you haven't seen your accountant you could be missing out on huge tax savings or growth opportunities for your company. Also, another benefit of year end planning is that you have most of your bookkeeping and balances established before the end of the year, saving time and heartache as the deadline approaches.

10. **Face the Music:**
    If you are behind on your bookkeeping, don't wait, get some help. Take your pile of receipts, your half-balanced accounts and find someone to straighten you out. If you

don't want to teach an employee how to do your books, hire your accountant to do your general ledger, expense tracking and financial statements. Figure it into your budget as a cost of doing business and appreciate the value in having it done right the first time. It will actually save you money in the long run. Accountants eat, sleep and breath to fix these messes in order to make it work for the business owner. They'll have looked at the numbers and be able to discuss with you monthly/quarterly/annually. The professional fees of these services are even tax deductible!

11. **Take Advantage of Tax Breaks:**
   Did you know as a small business owner, you may be able to hire your less than 18-year-old children, deduct their wages on your tax returns AND they don't have to file a tax return? What a great tax deduction because you are probably paying them anyway. I see a lot of small business owners not utilizing this great deduction, only because they don't know about it. This is only one of a thousand things that companies miss out on while trying to do everything on their own. Make the tax code work for you once in a while, just be sure to consult a professional and work within the law.

Having your own small business is one of the most difficult things you will endeavor. You need help to make things work. One of the best kept secrets is to use your accountant for more than just your income tax return preparation. If your current accountant is not interested in helping you with your business, maybe you should find a new accountant who specializes in your industry. Stop shuffling around the problem areas in your business. Seek help from professionals when you need them. Embrace doing weekly checkups on your financial well-being. These steps will help you to better protect and maintain your accounting health.

About Linda

Linda Trent, CPA graduated from high school in 1981 with a mission to become an accountant. During high school, accounting classes were her absolute favorite. While in college, after her undergrad work and starting on the upper division classes, her accounting professors were not too excited about teaching women. Accounting at that time was still very much a man's world.

Overcoming the industry's glass ceiling would be a challenge, but that never discouraged Linda because accounting was her passion. Linda's grandfather was an accountant and she endeavored to carry on the tradition. Senior year started out great and she soaked up the knowledge, but still had many factors stacked against her. Linda was in a very competitive accounting program where she was not in the highest rankings. She was not accepted to continue in the pursuit of an Accounting degree. Linda was forced to change her major to a general business degree. She believed this was the end of becoming an accountant.

With a general business degree, Linda became a loan officer at a local bank. Helping people get loans and watching their businesses become successful was very rewarding. While at the bank, she met a farmer. He was unfamiliar with creating his financial statements. This farmer was having trouble putting his budget together for a loan application, so Linda offered to help after banking hours. It was during those evenings that she realized she still wanted to be an accountant someday. This farmer really appreciated Linda's work and they had a lasting business relationship.

The connections made at the bank encouraged Linda to follow her true path. Patrons would come in and only want to speak with her, which frustrated the bank manager to the point where he fired Linda one day! Linda believed it was the worst day of her life. Devastated, she didn't know what to do but her husband had an accountant friend who needed some help, so she worked for him part time. Shortly thereafter, Linda started a bookkeeping company out of her home. With only the farmer as a client, he kept his business with her until he passed away.

Linda loved bookkeeping, she had found her purpose! She went back to college, worked her tail off for an accounting degree, tested for the CPA and in a flash, she had her license framed on the wall of her office. Linda and her husband bought the lot directly across the street from the bank that fired her, and she has been there for 30 years.

Being a banker was a wonderful experience that helped Linda plant roots in her small community. Hindsight is 20/20 and she is amazed by the way every single thing happens for a reason. Linda's true passion is accounting, learning how to collect the numbers and then using them to better understand a business is really remarkable. Over her career as a business owner, Linda has learned the value of expertise as well as how to face business challenges head on.

Contact information:
- office@trent-cpa.com

CHAPTER 3

"BUT IT'S DEDUCTIBLE!"

BY JON C. NEAL, CPA, MST, CPFP, CTP

So what? If I had a nickel for every time someone said that to me, I'd be richer than Bill Gates. I understand people are unhappy with government and want to do everything they can to minimize their taxes. But spending money just because you get a tax deduction is the WRONG way to do it. They don't realize a dollar spent is not a dollar in reduced taxes.

Let me give you an example. A business owner is in the 25% tax bracket. This means for every dollar of deductions, taxes are reduced by twenty-five cents. It still costs that business owner seventy-five cents out of his pocket to save twenty-five cents in taxes. Not a good deal. Many think it is even better if they borrow the money from the bank! After all, loan proceeds are not taxable, so you get the benefit of the deduction without having to pay taxes on the loan. What could be better?

Let me ask you a question, business owner. How are you going to pay that loan back? Another loan? You will have to generate profits in your business to pay the loan back, or even to get the loan in the first place. Focus on how to make money and keep it. This allows you to build wealth and not a house of cards – waiting for it to collapse. There are only four ways to make more money – raise prices, cut costs, get more customers and have your customers buy more from you. Let's look at some areas I find are good for cutting costs. Then, we will apply them to specific industries.

I. Accounting

First, let's look at what you pay for accounting services. Get the elephant out of the room. It sounds self-serving but most of the time you get what you pay for in bookkeeping, accounting and tax services. I know, "Jon, you're just saying that because it's your business." The important thing to remember here is what do you want to spend your time doing? Do you want to run payroll, file sales tax returns, or reconcile your bank account? Is your time better spent working on growing your business? What about those penalties you get for filing late or paying late? Many times they are more than the accounting fees you would have paid to get it done correctly. Think about it.

II. Insurance

Second, look over your insurance policies. In particular, look at your workers compensation policy. Even though the rates are established by your state and cannot be changed, there are wide variations with what you end up paying. First, look at how your employees are classified. For restaurants, a cook has a different rate from the manager or the bartender. In a construction company, a carpenter has a different rate than an estimator. Make sure your employees are classified correctly. Next, many insurance companies have discounts for different things you may already be doing. Do you hold monthly safety meetings? Do you have a safety manual? Boom! Discount. Next, look at your experience rating. This refers to how your company has done with work-related injuries. I have seen "mod factors" of .8, which means your premium is 80% of what the statutory premium is. Quite a savings, yes? Finally, shop around. Many insurance companies have programs for specific industries. Company A may love restaurants, Company B may decline a restaurant or have high premiums. Look at your liability coverage. Do you have enough? Do you have too much? Look at the cost of umbrella coverage, which is a means of covering some contingent liability. What about your property coverage? What would happen if a catastrophic event occurred? Would you be covered? Look at getting coverage for employee theft or dishonesty, business interruption coverage, internet coverage and employment practices. Sometimes an ounce of prevention is worth a pound of cure.

III. Advertising

Third, look at advertising. You need to analyze where you can get the biggest bang for your buck. Where do your customers hang out? What radio stations do they listen to? Do you really want to advertise your business on placemats for bingo at the church hall because it's cheap? Do your customers play bingo? There is a saying that you can only manage what you can measure. How do your customers find you? Do you ask them? Our customers often say, "I found you on the Internet." Where on the Internet? Google? Yelp? Streaming radio? How do you know what is working if you don't ask? I recommend using different tracking numbers for different ads or using codes to differentiate what medium is working. We ran the same radio ad on three different stations and used the code names of my grandchildren to track the station on which the caller heard the ad. When you do decide to advertise, negotiate! Everything is negotiable. Let's look at radio. You can negotiate the cost per spot, what time periods your ad runs, how many spots run per day or week, and extra spots. Maybe you need to be in the drive time hours but can get some bonus spots at other times of the day that work. You don't know until you try.

IV. Other Costs

Other areas to look at cutting costs include office supplies, operating supplies, and telephone service. Shop around and check prices and quality. Sometimes you can negotiate lower prices with local vendors by making them your sole provider for an item. Don't assume the big box chains are always lower. Look at buying in bulk for a discount. Just make sure you can use it up in a reasonable time period. Remember that generic is not always better than a brand name although it may seem cheaper at first glance. Using five rolls of generic paper towels at $1.00 each may be a bad deal if you can use two rolls of a brand name at $2.00 each. How many phone lines do you really need? Is internet phone service a good option?

Now, let's look at some industries and how to reduce costs.

Let's say you own a restaurant. Do you know what prime costs are? Do you know what **your** prime costs are? They are the costs associated with producing your product – food, beverage and labor. What are they supposed to be as a percentage of revenue? You should know. What do you do when cheese goes up $0.62 per pound, or tomatoes increase $1.25 per pound? If you don't keep track of costs you can't control what you keep. What are your portion sizes? Are there really two ounces of cheese in that taco? Could you save by using ten percent less? Is it worthwhile to use pre-portioned items in certain recipes? What is the real cost of those chicken wings? Did you include the sauce, the paper plate they are served on and the time making them? What about waste? How much of the steak is really "trimmed" and how much goes out the back door? Same thing with liquor. You started with 2 bottles of tequila, bought six and now have three left in stock. Your POS system says you sold two. Where did the other three bottles go? A good restaurateur has controls in place to provide information in all of these areas, allowing him or her to stay on top of costs and make the adjustments necessary to stay in business. Pit vendors against each other for price and quality. Look at changing the menu to eliminate low profit items or add new items at higher prices. How do you schedule your employees? Having ten employees clock in thirty minutes later saves you five hours per day. Look at the times of day and compare to employees working. Within reason, you may be able to reduce your staffing levels to coordinate with customer levels. Obviously, you can't send an employee home for thirty minutes in the middle of a shift.

Let's also look at contractors and how to reduce costs. The biggest problem I have seen is with specialty trades and supplies inventory. As an example, you have several plumbing trucks in your business, how often do you take an inventory of what is in those trucks? I had a client who had never taken an inventory of their trucks. They just kept ordering supplies when one of the employees said he didn't have an item. Maybe it rolled behind a shelf or was not in the correct place. Rather than look for it, he simply asked for more. When they finally took the inventory, they had enough of some items so they did not have to order them for a year! Inventory control is important.

The other area is not necessarily cost control but pricing the job appropriately. You are a masonry contractor. Your employees can lay 'x' bricks per hour. Pricing the job is easy, right? You estimate it will take 5,000 bricks to do the job. At the industry standard of 50 bricks per hour, the job should take 100 hours to complete. Material plus what you pay them, plus profit equals your price. Hold on! What about payroll taxes and workers compensation insurance? Oh! What about the employees having to unpack and pack their tools every day and the breaks which subtract one hour per day from laying the bricks? Now that job is going to take 125 hours to do. Industry averages are just that, averages. You need to look at your unique numbers and calculate your "average." Don't rely entirely on the industry association surveys or other sources of information.

You install wood floors. A salesperson visits you one day with a new brand of varnish. It is $1.50 per gallon cheaper than what you a using now. What a savings! Of course you sign up because it is going to save you money, right? But wait a minute. Your accountant tells you your labor costs are increasing as well as your supplies. That can't be. I am paying less for the varnish. I should be spending less, not more. What is going on? A deeper look finds the new varnish takes three coats rather than the two coats the old "expensive" varnish took. That means your employees are spending more time on the job as well. Suddenly the savings you thought you were going to get have gone up in smoke. Look before you leap!

In closing, remember it's not what you make, it's what you keep that counts. By looking at your numbers frequently and getting good advice to make decisions, you can keep more of what you work so hard to make. Yes, do what you can to take advantage of the tax laws in effect. Just don't go broke doing it.

About Jon

Jon Neal, CPA, MST, CPFP, CTP founded The Neal Group LLC in 1984. Jon has over 40 years of experience in public accounting. In 1977, he graduated from the University of Wisconsin-Milwaukee with a BBA in Accounting and Management Information Systems and in 1987 with a Master of Science in Taxation (MST).

Jon received his Certified Public Accountant (CPA) license in 1980 from the State of Wisconsin and is a member of the American Institute of Certified Public Accountants and the Wisconsin Institute of Certified Public Accountants. He is especially focused on closely-held businesses and their owners to help them reach their goals.

As a Certified Profit First Professional™ (CPFP) Jon works with businesses to keep more cash in their pockets. In addition to small business accounting, as a Certified Tax Professional® (CTP) Jon does extensive tax planning and tax resolution for individuals and businesses. He offers a free, no obligation thirty minute consultation to see if The Neal Group is the right fit for helping your business.

Jon is a best-selling author, having written four books on various topics and has appeared on various television and radio shows. Jon authored or co-authored the following books: *Best Doggone Financial Advice*, the best-selling *Breaking the Code, Obamacare and The IRS Uncovered* and *Doing Business in Wisconsin*.

Personally, Jon enjoys singing in his church's choir, spending time with his family and volunteer work. Jon and his wife, Ann, have four children and four grandchildren, and live in Hales Corners.

Contact:
- Email: jon@nealgroup.net

CHAPTER 4

WHY DIDN'T MY CPA TELL ME THAT?

BY CAROL WEEKLY

I seem to be having the same conversations over and over with small business owners that come to me by way of referral to handle their accounting needs. During our conversation I find that as small business owners, they are either a sole proprietor or an LLC.

Over the course of my 35+ years as a tax professional, I have learned a few things. One of the most important questions that is asked by my clients is, "How can I lower my tax bill?" The answer is simple, use the tax code or rules to your benefit.

The sad thing is that most people don't know how to take advantage of the tax codes or rules in order to minimize their taxes. So, what do they do? They go to a CPA after the year is over and they take their receipts and their 1099's or W-2's and the CPA puts all the numbers in the right spots and voila: here is your tax return and you owe this much money. Problem #1 is that going to a CPA or tax professional after the year is over is TOO LATE! Problem #2 is the CPA or the tax professional typically does not take the time to educate and inform the small business owner on how to effectively minimize their taxes.

Case in point: Nancy (names have been changed to protect the innocent), owns a small consulting firm. She is a one-woman show. Her attorney sets her up as an LLC. (Why an LLC when she doesn't have any assets in the business? I don't know. I have often wondered the same thing.)

She consults all year and earns a very nice net profit, after expenses, of a hundred thousand dollars. (I'll use $100k as an example so we can follow the numbers easily.) Nice job Nancy!

The time comes for her to take her records to her CPA, who then fills out a Schedule C. Oops! Wait, that is the same form that a Sole Proprietor fills out to do their taxes. Yes, it is. You see, a sole member LLC is treated the same as a Sole Proprietor for tax purposes – except in the State of California (which is where Nancy does her business). The State of California says, "Welcome to our state, you cute little LLC. Now, pay us $800 or more in California Franchise Tax Board minimum tax."

The only way for a single owner of an LLC (with no assets in the business) to avoid paying the minimum tax is to NOT be a single owner of an LLC (with no assets in the business)!

"Oh, but what about a Nevada or Delaware LLC? They don't have a state tax!" … you might say. Well, that is fine if your business resides in Nevada or Delaware or some other state. But if you have a Nevada or Delaware LLC and you conduct your business in California, California requires that you register your LLC in California as a Foreign LLC. The same rule applies to C or S Corporations. This will not avoid the minimum tax rule.

Let's get back to Nancy. Nancy's $100k net profit causes her to not only pay personal income tax based on her personal income tax bracket, but she will have to pay the same Self Employment Tax (or SE Tax) as if she didn't have the LLC in the first place.

The SE tax on $100k is $14,130 plus the $800 minimum tax to the State of California. Ouch!

Now, if we compare the $14,930 she paid to what she would have paid if she was in an S Corporation, she will have an entirely different outcome.

Assuming that Nancy is a single person with no dependents, her overall savings could be a whopping $14,255!

In some cities that could buy you a *vente-breve-vanilla latte* and a blueberry scone!

Now the question I then get after explaining this to my new client (of course all of my current clients take full advantage of the benefits of being properly structured for income tax purposes!) is: "WHY DIDN'T MY CPA TELL ME THIS?" And yes, they elevate their voices when they ask me that question and frankly, I can't blame them. I would want to know why a "CPA" who should know better, doesn't inform their clients of this strategy! But, even though it has been said that I can work miracles, I can't read minds and I can't figure out why CPA's allow their clients to over pay their tax bill.

You are probably at the point of: "Ok, Carol, that is great for Nancy, but how about me?"

I have great news for you. Here are the steps for applying the same strategy to your situation:

Step 1. Fire your CPA! No, I'm not kidding here. If your CPA has been allowing you to over pay your taxes, he or she should be fired.

Step 2. Hire a tax professional who is well versed in this strategy. Look for a tax professional who has the experience and knowledge and connections to make sure all the moving pieces are in place and run smoothly with minimal effort on your part.

Recommendation: Don't go cheap. Cheap is VERY expensive.

Step 3. After your new tax professional has connected you with the right contacts to setup your corporation and payroll and 401(k), focus on doing what you do best and leave the accounting and administrative tasks to those who are expert in their field. I sometimes find the need to explain to my new clients: "If I had to hire you to work in my accounting office, I'd have to pay you minimum wage because of your accounting skill level." Let me ask you: Would YOU work for minimum wage? Then don't attempt to do your own bookkeeping.

Here are some important tips on operating as a bonafide S-Corporation:

1. **Don't co-mingle your funds.** What I mean by this is that you should not use your corporate bank account as your personal spending account. This will destroy your "corporate veil." The easiest way to go around or under or simply ignore the corporate veil and the most vulnerable to attack is your bookkeeping and bank accounts. If anyone should want to sue you and you want to hide behind the "corporate veil", they simply will ask to see your bookkeeping records. If you have not treated your corporation as a corporation, why should they? Your corporation is a separate entity or separate being from your personal financial activities. It is as if you have given birth to a full-grown adult, without the labor pains of course! You wouldn't mix your personal money and frivolously spend your neighbor's money, would you? If you do or if you would, then you have more serious problems than I can fix.

2. **Pay yourself a regular reasonable salary**. In the creation of an S-Corp, you will be signing a form 2553, Election by a Small Business Corporation to elect to be recognized as an S-Corp. This form is sent to the Internal Revenue Service within 90 days of the formation of your corporation. You will receive a letter back from the Internal Revenue Service that tells you that your corporation is now recognized by them as a "flow-through" type of entity known as an S-Corp. In this letter you will be informed that you MUST receive wages and pay withholding taxes accordingly or your S-Corp status will be revoked. The Internal Revenue Service has not defined what is a "reasonable" salary is, but you should take your industry and skills into consideration when determining what your "reasonable" salary should be.

3. **Track your mileage.** This seems to be one of the expenses that most people are too lax about. First, it is a requirement that you keep a mileage log to write off your mileage, but people think it is too much to try to remember to write down where they go and how many miles they went from here to there. Well, with the app market explosion, we can easily solve this dilemma with apps on our phones that track our mileage for us. The one I like to use is MileIQ®. There are probably others out there, but this is the one I use, and I find it very easy. It automatically tracks all my mileage and allows me to easily categorize each trip.

You may be asking, "What if I want to do all of this myself, Carol? What are the detailed steps?"

Ok, you asked for it:

1. Select at least 3 names for your corporation. In case your first choice is taken you will still have a 2nd and a 3rd choice.

2. Decide how much of an investment you will make into your business. Many clients that I assist in setting up their

corporations, choose to value their stock at $1 per share and they set up the corporation with a $100 initial investment. This is a good amount to open a bank account with and a good amount to show as the "value" of your corporation, and this would be the amount "at risk."

3. Decide if anyone else will be joint shareholders in your corporation. This could be a strategy you could fit into your estate plan to avoid probate or inheritance tax. Of course, you would want to speak with your Certified Financial Planner regarding this choice.

4. Go to: www.mycorporation.com or to: www.legalzoom. com and fill out the online form(s). You can have them do everything from soup-to-nuts (I don't know where that saying came from), or you can pick and choose what they will do and what you will do.

5. If you choose to get your EIN (Employer Identification Number) yourself, it will be your corporate tax identification number, go to: www.irs.gov and click on the link to apply for an EIN. Follow the prompts and answer the questions.

   THIS IS VERY IMPORTANT: once you are assigned your EIN on the irs.gov website, be sure to **print** the page. Save this number. It is as important as your personal social security number. You will also receive a letter from the IRS with this number. You must wait for this letter before you go to the bank to open an account as outlined below in step 7.

6. Google "corporate kits" to find and order a corporate binder kit to put all your important corporate documents in.

7. Once your Articles of Incorporation arrive from the Secretary of State, you can take this document along with your EIN letter from the Internal Revenue Service and a "Corporate Resolution for Banking" to the bank to open your corporate bank account or accounts.

8. Contact a payroll provider to set yourself up to receive payroll wages on a regular basis.

9. Work with a financial advisor to set up a 401(k) retirement fund to maximize the tax savings benefit for retirement funding. The contribution limits are much greater in a 401(k) than in a traditional IRA.

10. Hire an experienced bookkeeper and tax professional to make sure that your accounting is kept up-to-date on a weekly basis, and that your estimated taxes and payroll withholdings are appropriate for your income.

Here is one last piece of advice:
NEVER *allow your bookkeeper or accountant or tax professional to have signing authority on your bank accounts. No matter who they are.*

Lastly, I'd like to answer the question: When is it appropriate to operate as an LLC instead of an S-Corp? If you have "active" income from a business, then an S-Corp is the appropriate entity from a tax perspective. The beauty of the tax advantages lies within the S-Corp.

If you have "passive" income from investments, then an LLC may be the entity for you. An LLC is not a tax-saving entity or strategy. It is for protecting assets.

In the book written by Mark J. Kohler, *Lawyers are Liars*, Mark explains the strategies that work to protect our assets and uses more than 270 footnotes to do it, quoting and referencing the true experts around the country. I highly recommend reading this book.

I hope this chapter has given you a little insight into why and how an S-Corp can help you *Keep-It!*

About Carol

Carol Weekly has spent the last 35+ years assisting small business owners and individuals navigate the complex world of tax returns. She has helped clients save from tens of thousands to hundreds of thousands of dollars in tax savings, as well as discovering and uncovering missed tax-saving opportunities.

Carol's clientele ranges from real estate agents to small construction companies, from lawyers and doctors to consultants, actors, directors, executives and wage earners.

Her clients sometimes say, "If there is one thing Carol knows, it's everything!" Carol doesn't know everything, but what she does know, she generously shares with everyone who cares to benefit from it. Carol's expertise comes from continuing to educate herself in the area of taxation and from having a fine sense of how to care about the client as an individual.

Carol has successfully negotiated with the IRS to settle an account for 4 cents on the dollar as she helps clients resolve issues with different taxing authorities. Carol has clients from Alaska and Hawaii to Florida and New York.

Carol has clients who have been with her for over 20 years, begging her not to leave them. Carol takes all of her own advice and "walks the talk" with her own S-Corporation.

You can contact Carol at:
- carol@carisenterprises.com

CHAPTER 5

KEEP YOUR MONEY AND SAVE ON TAXES

BY JENNIFER ALLEN, CPA, MBA

I meet with a lot of clients who want to save tax dollars and all they think about doing is going out and buying equipment or a new car. Those ideas are good if you really need the equipment/supplies you are buying. What if I told you there were some ways to save tax dollars and keep your money? Does that sound like a better idea than going out and getting a truck loan or buying things just to have them? Here are a few of my ideas and how they can help you.

HEALTH SAVINGS ACCOUNTS (HSA)

I feel that this is the most underutilized tax benefit available today and that is for the self-employed as well as employees. This is how they work at the very basic level. You have a high deductible HSA eligible health insurance plan (you will know because it will say it in the plan type). You need this plan type to open an HSA account. You can fund up to $6,900 for a family and $3,450 for an individual per year for 2018. (2019: $7,000 and $3,500.) If you are over 50, you get to make an additional $1,000 catch-up contribution and if your spouse is also over 50 you can do an additional catch-up contribution for him/her.

Any contribution you make to your HSA account is a deduction on page 1 of your individual tax return just like a traditional IRA. When you take distributions they are tax free, including earnings, like a Roth IRA, assuming you use the money for qualified medical expenses. It sounds simple but here is where it can be a huge benefit.

1) Health care/health insurance is not going down in price. If you have shopped for health insurance, the least expensive are the high deductible plans. If you and your family are generally healthy you can save money on premiums with these plans. They still cover routine preventative healthcare just like the other plans but if you have a catastrophic event you will have the higher deductibles to meet. This is where the HSA account steps in. For the years when you only have minor medical expenses, the money in the HSA account accumulates. If a tragic event happens, that accumulated money will step in and pay the deductibles.

2) To make the high deductible plan work the HSA account must be open. If you don't have the money to fully fund in the current year, you should open the account with whatever you have. The rule: funds in an HSA account can be used for any qualified medical expense incurred AFTER the account is OPENED. For example, suppose that in January 2018 you went with the high deductible insurance and opened the HSA account with $50. Later that year there was an accident and you ended up with $4,000 in medical bills out of pocket. You can take the $4,000 you owe and make an HSA contribution in 2018. You can then immediately take the money out of the account and pay the medical bills. Here is the benefit – your bills were not high enough to qualify for the medical deduction on the Schedule A, but you do get to take the page 1 deduction for the $4,050 in HSA contributions for 2018. If you are self-employed, you get to take the self-employed health insurance deduction as well.

3) You go with the high deductible health insurance and you are blessed to never need to use it except for routine health care. You are also able to fully fund the HSA account every year. If you open the account at an institution that offers underlying investments, you will be required to keep a certain amount in cash and then invest the rest. They will offer a menu of mutual funds to choose from and depending on your risk tolerance, you can put the money in mutual funds to grow just like a Roth IRA. This is what it can look like for a family plan. For ease of calculation, I am going to assume an annual contribution of $7,000 starting at age 40 and going until age 65 when Medicare kicks in and you can no longer contribute to an HSA.

FAMILY PLAN
$7,000 (annual contribution) x 25 years = $175,000 in tax deductible contributions
$175,000 + $128,182 (tax-free earnings on investments at 4%) = $303,182 account balance at retirement

INDIVIDUAL PLAN
$3,500 (annual contribution) x 25 year = $87,500 in tax deductible contributions
$87,500 + $64,091 (tax-free earnings on investments at 4%) = $151,591 account balance at retirement

This is a very conservative estimate with earnings at 4% but we must consider the down years and the fact that you just might need the money before retirement and there is no calculation for the tax savings. I also assumed that the contributions would never increase for simplicity. The reality is the contribution limits are indexed and increase every year. In addition, there is the catch-up contributions at age 50 (an additional $30,000 for family, $15,000 for individual). Even if it stayed the same, I would be happy to have $303,000 to pay for my healthcare after retirement.

4) No one says that you must pay for your medical expenses from this account. You have enough cash flow to fully fund the account and are still able to pay for the medical expenses out-of-pocket. You like the idea in the above investment scenario and want to let those funds grow. However, you do have annual out-of-pocket medical expenses of $2,500 that you have been able to budget for. You can pay the $2,500 and save that bill in a "not reimbursed by HSA" file. That starts in 2018 and goes until 2043 (25 years). You have a file with $62,500 in medical expenses that ARE ELIGIBLE to be reimbursed through the HSA. At age 65 you want to take an around-the-world vacation, so you take the "not reimbursed by HSA" file and submit for reimbursement. You get $62,500 in tax-free medical reimbursement from the $303,182/$151,591 balance in the account. There is no restriction on the time to take the reimbursement. The only rule is that the expense must be incurred AFTER the HSA account is opened.

5. Qualified medical expenses include anything that is deductible on the Schedule A (Itemized Deductions) except for health insurance premiums. The exception to this rule is Long Term Care insurance. Those premiums can be paid from this account. To see all the eligible medial expenses please visit: www.irs.gov and refer to IRS Publication 502 "Medical and Dental Expenses." I would list them here except they change, and you want to make sure you have the most accurate list. If you take a withdraw for an ineligible expense, there is a 20% penalty and it is taxed at your ordinary income tax rate.

Based on the information I have provided, I hope you can see the benefits of the HSA and can figure out how to make it work for you. There are a lot of other things that you can do with these accounts when it comes to employees and offering a benefits package.

RETIREMENT ACCOUNTS

These accounts are more common but under-utilized. There are so many options to choose from for every person/organization to fit with the funds that are available. Again, you can save tax dollars and save money – Win/Win! Here are the types of accounts and how they can benefit you and your business.

I. <u>Traditional and Roth IRA (Individual Retirement Account)</u>

These accounts are the easiest to open/manage and a great place for someone who is just starting out. The maximum contribution is earned income up to a maximum of $5,500 with a catch-up contribution of $1,000 if you are over 50. There are some rules including but not limited to: earned income from self-employment or W2s and phase-out for deductibility based on income. The due date to open an account and make the contribution is the due date of the tax return including extensions. (Exp. 2018 tax return due in April 2019 can be extended until October 2019 and the 2018 contribution would need to be made by then.)

II. <u>IRA</u>

These are tax deductible in the year the contribution is designated. At age 70½, you will be required to make a distribution.

If you are limited to the amount of contribution, then it will be reclassified to a Non-deductible IRA and will be handled differently on distribution. (Please consult your tax advisor for details.)

III. <u>Roth</u>

These contributions are NOT tax deductible but grow tax-free and all distributions after 59½ are tax free.

There is no required minimum distribution.

If you are limited to the amount of contribution, you can make a "back-door" Roth. It can be a little complicated but here are basic the steps:

- o You cannot have another IRA account open with funds to make this work perfectly.
- o You make a non-deductible traditional IRA contribution.
- o Immediately make a Roth conversion – roll the money from the IRA to the Roth.
  - • If you have another IRA account, the Roth conversion will not be 100% unless you convert all your funds which can create a taxable event. It is a proportional rollover and will make part of the contribution non-deductible IRA and the other part Roth. You want to avoid this situation! It might be appropriate to convert all your funds and would be worth a conversation with your tax preparer.
- o Do not report the IRA contribution as deductible on your tax return.

When deciding which type of account to open you need to consider your future income needs and tax situation. The IRA will be taxed when withdrawn and the Roth will be tax-free.

IV. SIMPLE IRA (Savings Incentive Match Plan for Employers)

The first two accounts are designed for individuals but can be used by businesses. The SIMPLE is designed for employers (sole-proprietors, partnerships, S-Corporations, C-Corporations) and is a great way to offer an employee benefit without creating a financial burden to the business. They are easy to open and manage. There is a plan contract and each employee who participates will need to open an account, but management fees are low and charged to the participant not the employer. There are no additional reporting requirements as there are with 401(k) plans. Here

is how they work for you and your employees:
- The maximum employee contribution for 2018, which is withheld pre-tax from their paycheck, is $12,500 with a $3,000 catch-up contribution if you are over 50.
- The employer match is equal to the employee contribution not to exceed 3% of the participants salary/wage.
  - An employee whose gross wages are $50,000 and elects to make the maximum contribution of $12,500, the maximum employer contribution (your expense) will be $1,500 ($50,000 @ 3%).
  - An employee who elects to have 1% withheld of $50,000 in wages ($500) then the employer contribution will only be $500. You cannot exceed the employee's contribution.
- Employees must participate to get the match.

If you want to start offering your employees a benefit, this is a great plan to begin. You also know that the employee has an investment in there as well.

V. SEP IRA (Simplified Employee Pension)

These accounts are designed for the sole-proprietor though they can be used if you have employees. Your annual contribution is based on the net income from your business or wages. The maximum is 25% of the net income/wages up to $55,000 for 2018. (There is a modification for self-employed, but the maximum is still the same. Your tax preparer will help you with the final maximum based on your situation.)

If you have employees and you contribute to your own account, you must contribute to their account. There is no employee participation only employer.

- You are an employee of your business and your

wages are $60,000, your SEP contribution will be $15,000.
- You have (x) employees that each make $40,000 plus your wages of $60,000, the total SEP contribution will be $35,000 and divided proportionally between the accounts.

The employee owns their account and can take a distribution at any time after funding (subject to all penalties and taxes based on age and reason) and have no personal money in the account. You do not have to fund every year and it does not have to be the full 25%. You just must remember what you do for one, you do for all.

VI. 401(k) Plans
There are a few different types, but I want to talk briefly about the Solo (Single) K and the Safe Harbor 401(k). If you want to offer a 401(k), I recommend talking with your tax professional and/or financial advisor for more detailed information. These plans can get as complicated as you want or need them to be.

VII. Solo or Single K
This is a great plan for the solo-practitioner or the husband/ wife team who have no other employees. You get all the benefits of the 401(k) with a profit-sharing contribution.

- Maximum pre-tax payroll deduction (2018) per individual is $18,500 with a $6,000 catch-up contribution if over 50.
- Maximum employer profit sharing is 25% of gross wages.
- Total retirement contributions max out at $55,000 (2018).

If you do not take a paycheck because you file as a Schedule C (Sole-Proprietor), you still get the generous contributions with a slightly different calculation for the profit-sharing portion. Your tax advisor should be able to provide you with the maximum contribution in your unique situation.

This plan does not have the same testing rules and other management rules of the traditional 401(k), but when the account reaches $250,000 there is a Form 5500EZ filing requirement. Be sure to check with your tax advisor for other rules that might apply.

VIII. <u>Safe Harbor 401(k)</u>

This is the last step before the traditional 401(k). This is designed for the small to medium-size business who wants to offer a larger benefit than the SIMPLE can offer but avoid the non-discrimination testing of the traditional 401(k).

- o Maximum pre-tax payroll deduction (2018) per individual is $18,500 with a $6,000 catch-up contribution if over 50.
- o Employer Contribution (you, the business owner, are an employee for this type of account):
  - Dollar-for-dollar matching contribution for participating employees up to 4% of participant wages.

    OR
  - Contribute 3% of compensation for each eligible employee regardless of participation.
- o Total retirement contributions max out at $55,000 (2018) per employee.

When this account reaches $250,000, there is a Form 5500EZ filing requirement. Be sure to check with your tax advisor for other rules that might apply.

I hope that you will be able to implement a tax savings plan that keeps your dollars in your pocket!

About Jennifer

Jennifer Allen, CPA, MBA, thrives on helping her clients create a secure financial future. From traditional tax planning to individual and business financial coaching, her goal with each client is to create a strong financial base so they can grow and thrive in this ever-changing environment.

Jennifer graduated from West Virginia Wesleyan College with a finance degree. After getting a seasonal position during tax season, she determined that tax preparation was the career path she would pursue. To become a Certified Public Accountant (CPA), she needed additional hours. She obtained her master's in Business Administration (MBA) from Mount Saint Mary's University (formerly Mount Saint Mary's College). Once she had her MBA she went on to sit for the CPA exam while working full-time for a private accounting practice. After 13 years working with a very experienced accountant in tax, she decided she wanted to do something that was not so traditional.

Jennifer started her own tax practice with the help of her parents. Meeting with clients, she discovered that there was a need for people to have a financial advisor, but not in the traditional investing way. This advisor would be able to answer questions from budgeting to borrowing and planning to retirement. She obtained her advisory license and insurance license to learn the ins-and-outs of these fields.

Today, Jennifer offers all traditional tax services as well as being a Master Financial Coach. She speaks to small business groups about new tax laws and to groups of individuals about the basic of budgeting. She also advises both groups about living/working without debt, debt repayment and saving to work without debt.

CHAPTER 6

KEEP MORE OF WHAT YOU EARN

BY CLIFFORD BENJAMIN

Are you a Sole practitioner? Are you the one who makes ALL of the decisions in your business? When it comes to your business, do you feel like you are a One-Man-Band? In other words, "The music don't get played unless I play it." If that's you, then this is for you.

I specialize in helping those that feel like they are always the point of the spear, or the "One-man-band"; if you recognize that feeling then you are going to love this. First, let me reassure you that there is hope. You really can get off the merry-go-round of constantly being bombarded by problems. You can stop being the fireman that has to put out all the fires, and start being the person that you visualized that you would be when you first started your business.

Do you find yourself working harder and putting in more hours, and asking yourself...

- "Where's the money?"
- "Why do we have less money than last year?"

So, you then engage in working harder and longer.

The answer to your questions is **Cash leaks!** Cash is leaving your business faster than you are bringing it in.

The good news, if you will, is that you are not alone. The bad news is that most businesses suffer from one or more of these cash leaks. In fact, 7 out of 10 businesses that fail do so because of cash flow leaking from their businesses. Many businesses experience a 50% cash flow loss. That's why we will be discussing how you can stop the leaks and keep more.

Most businesses are leaking cash like a sieve. It brings to mind an image of the business person as a One-Man-Band in an old, leaky row boat.

If you can just take a moment, visualize an overworked, overstressed One-Man-Band in an old, leaky row boat. He is so busy playing to keep cash coming in that he is too busy to bail. And he cannot stop playing and he cannot bail. He is sinking. To make matters worse, the motor on the back of the boat is smoking; it's not going to take him anywhere! And to make matters even worse, there is a storm on the horizon heading his way! He is really in trouble now.

Now hopefully this poor guy does not reflect how badly your business is operating. However, you might relate to one or more of his dilemmas.

Now, you might relate to this business person. This person starts his business to do something that he liked to do, and to provide for his family so that he could enjoy spending time with them as his children were growing up. He knew that it might be a struggle to start and run a business, but he thought it will be worth it, "because I'll be my own boss and be able to provide for my family and spend time with them as they grow." But, what happened? The struggle never got better, it was always a struggle. Why was that? He might have thought: "Oh well, it will get better if I just work longer and harder. So longer and harder became the norm and now the kids are grown, the wife and I are older, but I am still working my butt off. We don't have enough money to retire, so now I really have to work harder and more!"

Ah, the sweet trap. How did I get here? How do I escape? Now what? Well, for some of you the game is almost over.

Does that matter? Are you going to give up or continue? I have to continue! Now what?

Ok! So, let's stop the hemorrhaging of cash from your business so that you can keep more of it. Here comes the place for the not-so-good news. The solution is normally an easy fix, you're just not 'gonna' like it, but YOU 'gotta' do it.

If you want to keep more of what you are earning, then YOU must realize that you are leaking cash and if you want to keep more of it, there is one thing that you must do. Take control of your cash flow. What this means is that whomever you have hired or appointed to manage the business check book must be on your side and on the same page as you are.

If that IS the case now, then YOU are the problem. If not, then your keeper of the check book is the problem.

I have seen the keeper of the check book be:

- the owner's wife
- a girlfriend
- the secretary
- or even the cleaning lady

Now, they may be very accomplished, however most of the time they are not trained or experienced enough to realize that cash is leaking out of your business, sorry. Money is slipping through their fingers and flying out the door.

It may not be big things, but little things have a way of adding up quickly. But, whatever it is, you are not keeping it!

For example, as I walked into the office of one of my clients, I noticed that his receptionist, secretary, bookkeeper, girl Friday, girlfriend was readying a quantity of small packages to be mailed out. There might have been about forty or so small boxes, which she was getting ready to mail. I watched for a while and asked her what she was doing. She said that she was preparing the packages to take to the post office. She had already sealed and labeled them and was in the process of weighing each of them and putting stamps on them. I asked her if she did this often, Oh yes, at least twice a week, sometimes more. I then asked her if she was aware of a service the post office offers, where the post office will pick up all the packages from the office and take them to the post office where they will weigh and put the correct postage on them and bill you once a month – thereby saving her the time and expense of weighing and putting postage on them and then loading them into her car and transporting them to the post office and having to make several trips from her car to the post office to take the packages in. She said that she was not aware of that service, but it doesn't matter anyway because that is NOT how SHE does it. Can you believe the audacity of her spending all that time and money when it could be done by the post office for free? I see things like this every day where cash is being shoveled out the front door; it is unbelievable how people waste time and money. And you are paying for it. Wouldn't you rather keep that money and take your family somewhere?

The loss of cash is not usually intentional; it's that they just do not realize the effect of their actions. They think that they are doing the right thing. However, I have also seen many, many cases of embezzlement, even by family members.

Now the good news is that it is an easy fix. If you don't know how, I am sure that you can find an accountant that can help you. The most important thing is that YOU must become involved, and not let some else do it for you. YOU must do a weekly review of the books and have a management review of the books every month. I cannot tell you how important this can be. I know an accountant, an accountant who had to file bankruptcy, and he chose to file chapter 11 reorganization. This calls for a monthly operating report to be filed with the trustee every month. Now his wife was his bookkeeper and keeper of the check book. Now fortunately for him, his wife was very good and trustworthy. She was not the reason for his bankruptcy. However, since he knew that she was capable and trustworthy, he only looked at the books at tax time when he prepared the return. Everything seemed to be ok.

Now the Chapter 11 trustee began asking for monthly operating reports for both business and personal accounts with a full reconciliation down to the last penny. The first month that they had to prepare the reports and reconcile the bank accounts from both to a consolidated report, they almost got divorced. Not really, but it was not pretty. After a few stressful months they had worked out a system so now what took hours and a lot a stress could now be completed in about an hour with both of them working together. They ended up being much closer due to the process.

He later told me that he had thought that he was being a good business man running his business like he should. However, when he was doing the monthly reports he learned a great deal about his business and himself. He is now much more relaxed and comfortable in his business, and his business is doing much better now that he reviews the business reports every month. He uses this review as a management tool to run his business. He is making more money, has a larger bank balance and is not stressed. He IS keeping more!

As an added benefit, your partner Uncle Sam will be happy that you are keeping good records and you will be even happier because you will be keeping more cash and have a complete record of all of your deductions for your tax return. Everybody wins. You are happy and not so stressed, your family is happy to see more of you, your tax man is happy, and you can keep Uncle Sam happy. And you will end up keeping more what you earned!

I have worked with most every type of business from Chiropractor to MD, Insurance agent, Attorney, Real Estate Broker, General Construction Contractor, HVAC contractor, Pet Shop, Gun Shop, Machine shop, Marina, Restaurant, Bars, Tree Farm, Chicken Farm to you-name-it. I have probably worked with at least one of them over the past 40 years.

For the most part, they all have several things in common. Since I tend to work mainly with small businesses or Sole Practitioners, I get to be really friendly and "hands on" with the owner and staff. Over the years I have seen so much that it is second nature for me to perform an audit whenever I walk in to most any business. I can immediately begin to identify several areas of concern. The following is just one example of how I was able to assist a business man keep more of his earnings.

After speaking with the owner for a bit, I discovered that a great deal of his cash is leaking out of his business through loan payments. He had too much debt. Does this sound familiar? Then this will help you keep more. Other than tax savings strategies, this one concept may be the number one method for you to keep more of what you earn.

Usually there are credit card, auto loan, mortgage and student loans. These are all very different types of loans, and he was, of course, paying the minimum payment on all of them and wondering why they were not getting paid off. So, if he happens to get a little ahead in the business he wants to pay down the debt. Great! How do we do that? Most folks do it the absolutely worst way. Let's say that they have an extra $1500 to pay down debt, great you say. Not so fast, how are you 'gonna' decide who gets what? Most folks say, well we have 10 loans so let's spread it around evenly and pay $150 on each one, right? Wrong. Most folks do not even know that there actually is a mathematical formula to determine which loan or loans to pay down first. So, they just spread it around evenly. This is more cash leaving a sinking ship, and less for you to keep.

The formula which is used to determine which loan to pay extra on is:

DIVIDE THE CURRENT LOAN BALANCE BY THE MINIMUM PAYMENT.

This yields a number, which is an indicator as to which loan will free up the most cash flow when you make an extra payment to it.

The lower the indicator number the more cash that will be freed up by paying more on it. So, you can make a little spreadsheet to calculate the indicator for every month if you wish. Place all your loan balances in one column and the minimum payment in another adjacent column, then divide the current loan balance by the minimum payment, placing the results in a third column. Then look at the indicator numbers in the indicator column. If you should have a few extra bucks to pay on as loan, you can select the one with the lowest number and pay ALL on it. This way you will be keeping more cash flow by paying down on the loan that yields the best results. Here is a tip: Let's say that you have been making a minimum payment of $100 per month and you finish paying off the loan. Then you take that same $100 that you had been paying on that retired loan and use it to pay an extra $100 per month on the next loan that is indicated by the formula. This is called Rollup. If you keep rolling up from one loan to the next you will be amazed at how quickly that all of the loans will be paid off, thereby increasing what you get to keep.

The good news is that if the owner is willing he can identify and cure most of what ails the business, but it takes work, commitment, knowledge and determination to cure all of the ills.

Get good competent help to assist you in finding and curing these cash flow leaks so that you will have more to keep.

This has been about how to keep the cash that comes into the business. Now that you have gained some control over the cash flow, you can begin to address the other monetary issues in your business. For example, how to scale your business to make more and keep more, wealth accumulation, retirement, legacy and Taxes.

So now, instead of being a One-Man-Band in a leaky row boat, you can now be the Captain of your own ship. I see you sitting up high in the Captain's chair of a 75-foot motor launch, while the band is playing on the lower deck. There are no more leaks and the sea is smooth and it is clear sailing from here on.

SO, KEEP ON KEEPING ON!

GOOD LUCK!

About Clifford

Clifford Benjamin is a solutions-oriented Senior Executive with more than 50 years of success across the tax, accounting, insurance and firearm industries. Leveraging extensive experience providing entrepreneurial coaching and tax services for various companies, he is a valuable advisor for from start-ups to medium-sized businesses needing guidance with making informed financial decisions, and the proper understanding of revenue and assets placement, to assure that the tax burden is minimized.

His broad areas of expertise include due diligence, management consulting, income tax preparation, tax solutions, and tax debt relief. His exceptional ability to develop rapport quickly enables him to provide support and strategic financial advice under often stressful situations.

Throughout his career, he has held leadership positions with Ben's Coin & Gun shop, Inc., Management South, Accurate Tax & Accounting, Max Refunds Express, Express Tax of America, Inc., Better Firearms Design, Inc. and White Tiger Financial.

Contact information:
- Tel: 386-257-1040
- Email: MaxRefundsExpress@gmail.com
- Website: www.MaxrefundsExpress.com

CHAPTER 7

GOAL-SETTING STRATEGIES FROM THE GRIDIRON
HOW TO WIN BIG IN LIFE, FINANCES & ENTREPRENEURSHIP

BY BRETT S. PARKER

It's no secret. Life can be hard. And what some would consider being even harder is starting and growing a successful small business. But with a clear vision, the right education, and confidence in proper goal-setting, the path to entrepreneurship doesn't have to be so intimidating. You can keep your commitment to family time and manage your finances effectively while you build your business. Much like winning in a football game, success in life is dependent upon doing a few things well – like outworking the competition and having a strong team that you can rely on.

I understand the fears that can come up in someone's thoughts when they are considering starting a business – whether it's important questions from, "How do I go about starting?" or "Am I going to be successful?" to ultimately, the question that it all leads to, "Am I handling my taxes and financials correctly?"

HOW TO MAKE WHAT YOU NEED AND WANT THE SAME THING

I can speak to those concerns because I have been there too. Not only have I started a business, but prior to this, I was in the corporate sector, as a lead sales agent. I've done sales, and I've really been through the ups and downs of starting and growing a business. I didn't come into business with a silver spoon. My mom and dad weren't rich. I did all this from just muscling my way through. And eventually, it allowed me to leave my job. So really, it is just sharing that message that if I can do it, anybody can do it. When I meet with clients, I tell them, "Let's figure out how to make what you need and what you want the same thing."

When I do a consultation with clients, I'll ask them, "If I gave you a magic wand for life and asked you to use it to paint your own picture of how things would look if everything were perfect, what would your picture look like? What's the house you want, the car you want? What would you want your family to be like? Let's get clear on what that perfect version of life would look like." And after they paint that picture, we just come back and begin breaking down the goals necessary to turn that dream into a reality.

THE KEY TO CONFIDENCE IS FOCUSED GOAL-SETTING & EDUCATION

Success in entrepreneurship, family, and every other aspect of life, is found in effectively setting and achieving regular goals. Reaching small goals give you the confidence to tackle larger ones. This increased confidence allows you to learn more and build upon your current knowledge base, which in turn gives you more confidence.

When it comes to effective goal setting, I've found that it's better to focus on individual elements rather than trying to focus on

70

working on everything as a whole. What I coach clients to do, is to focus on 2 – 4 items either monthly or quarterly, and just pound those out. Don't do anything else until those few items have been completed. And then we just keep building from there, month after month. We also do confidence exercises, where we build their confidence and make it stronger by having faith in the plan.

OVERCOMING OBSTACLES THROUGH EDUCATION

We're all going to experience obstacles and setbacks along the way. But the thing that matters most is how we respond to those setbacks, and how we make a plan for overcoming the obstacles and other challenges that will inevitably come up with starting and growing a successful business. When you have a vision that you are passionate about, as well as belief and confidence in your abilities, then it's just a matter of getting the right education that's necessary to be successful.

Throughout my life, I've always had my mind focused. No matter what I'm selling or who I'm working with, whether it's coaching clients in finance, growing a business or coaching kids in the basics of football skills, I am always focused on building their confidence and knowledge for them to reach their dreams.

FOOTBALL'S METAPHOR FOR LIFE AND BUSINESS

I played football for a long time. And early on, I had a coach tell me, even though there are eleven guys on a team, we all wore the same jersey, and we were all playing together for the same goal, to win the game. And that is just like life. We have to figure out where you fit on the team. You know, are you a great thinker or are you a great doer? What are your skills? It's the same thing in football. Different people have different skills and strengths, but where do they fit on the team? And that's how life is, we're all on one big team. So where do you fit in society? Where can you help for the greater good of the world?

Football is also a lot like life and business. Even before you are on the field, you know a game may only be 2 to 3 hours, but nobody sees the 12 to 15 hours of practice before the game. No one sees the offseason workouts. Everyone watches on game day and what you see is the finished product. But the fans in the audience rarely see all the long hours and hard work spent during time in practice.

COACHING TIPS FROM THE TEAM CAPTAIN

Once you're on the field or running your own business, it all comes down to delegating tasks and responsibilities. What I learned early on, being a football captain, is how to approach different people. I can't just go to someone with a big 'rah, rah' motivational speech that says, "Let's go do this and no excuses!" Some people need a little more explanation or more guidance in their work. You just can't treat everyone the same.

That's why I've never put out a cookie-cutter type approach to planning or with a speaking assignment that I give. I believe everything needs to be customized to the specific needs of the individual or organization.

HOW TO PREPARE FOR THE CHALLENGE

You take risks to start your own business. There is a lot of uncertainty that may require you to become comfortable with the uncomfortable. Life's not easy! How I approached it was to set out to enjoy the ride. At the other end of the tunnel was some light. I always kept in mind that I'm not out here operating without a purpose.

I tell people to embrace the change. And let's come up with a solid enough plan to ensure the transition to entrepreneurship isn't as difficult as the one I went through. I didn't really have a plan. I was just out there. My business started out as a side-hustle, and then all of a sudden, it took off. So now I am a big advocate of being proactive and not reactive.

THE IMPORTANCE OF FAMILY

Entrepreneurship is very difficult. You can't prepare for everything, but you can prepare well enough that you'll be ready for anything. I tell individuals, let's plan for uncertainty. So, it's a good idea to explain to your spouse or significant other that there may be times where you have to work long hours when you are getting started, or that there may be ups and downs in the bank account. But it all goes back to planning and making sure that everyone is on board ahead of time.

My family is everything to me. They are my "why". I have three kids and the only time I may miss something is during tax season. For people going into business for themselves, they really need to figure out what role their family plays in that whole process. Your family is going to be there if it pops or if it flops. And I feel that people in business think that they have to choose between their work and their family, and that simply is not true. It's not either/or. When it really comes down to it, it just goes back to some baseline experiences with planning. If you plan right, then you can execute better, and it's a lot less stress on everybody.

PRACTICAL TIPS ON TAXES AND FINANCES

I encourage people who are considering starting a business to plan and save up about a year-and-a-half of lifestyle needs, plus 15% to 20%. That way there's no reduction in the standard of living while you're getting the business going. I also encourage them to eliminate or reduce debt. And don't forget to save some money for "You time" for yourself, or for a vacation with your spouse and family. Don't just plan on how to pay the bills, but also add in some exciting time and some date money for you and the spouse. It's definitely required for the journey to have a budget for that exciting time stashed away with your savings.

If you are a business owner, you really should hire someone who specializes in tax matters to figure out what type of business you're going to do and identify the maximum number of deductions that you can take. Leave no stone unturned. Take all the deductions you can. I see very high numbers of small business that don't take advantage of simple deductions. Look at things like how to travel for business and do business meetings over lunches or dinners. Check out things like how to claim uniform expenses, and other things like that – which are day-to-day expenses – but you can't take advantage of them if you aren't educated.

GAME PLAN FOR YOUR ACCOUNTING

Here's a typical story that I see playing out everyday in my practice: A new entrepreneur decides to set out and achieve their dream of becoming a business owner. But right from the start, they are unsure what kind of business entity they are and they are unaware of the potential tax implications. So, they file as a corporation in order to appear larger to the outside world. Now, fast-forward 365 days, and they are preparing for tax season. They think that just because they have kept most of their receipts that they can just deduct their expenses from revenue. But they find out that the new tax form is a little more complicated than what they are used to. They try to fill it out as best they can and hope for the best. And then, bam! Six weeks later, they get a certified letter from the IRS telling them they're going to be audited.

Talk about a stressful situation! Yet this is something I handle in my office on a regular basis. It's typical that new business owners wear many hats. Along with being the owner and manager, they also try to play accountant in an attempt to save money. However, this can actually have a negative affect on finances because they

74

usually don't have the tax knowledge to keep accurate records. And while no one wants to deal with going through an IRS audit, there are some basic steps you can take to be as prepared as you can be:

1) **The Play!** The first step to helping with audit prevention is business entity selection. Each entity has different tax advantages and disadvantages. Hiring a professional to assist with this step is imperative to the success of your business

2) **The Best Teammate You Can Pick.** Hiring someone with tax knowledge is essential. Besides, just with taxes, a great financial person can keep you up to date with various changes in the law or with updates on the financial health of the business and provide overall peace of mind knowing that the bloodline of your business is being taken care of.

3) **Being Prepared.** Having proof of your financial actions is very important – not just what you made, but also what you spent. Yearly, the IRS and other local taxing authorities send out letters requesting explanations for income and expenses. I advise clients to have a plan in place to handle the record keeping as if they are operating at their goal-pace, and not just a beginner's pace. Good record keeping isn't just making sure you have it, but also knowing where to find those records when necessary.

4) **Going on Time!** When running a business, you are required to file with different agencies at different times throughout the year. What and when to report can vary depending on your industry and business entity you are classified under. Also, as I mentioned before, industry and entity classification can play a major key in what taxes your business will have to pay. Filing on time is very, very important. Not filing on time can have a major effect on your business, and in some instances, can even cause your business to be shut down until the issue is addressed and resolved.

I don't want these things to scare you. I want to see you follow your dreams. But I also want to make you aware of some of the key areas that I have seen in my career in serving business owners that can lead to negative issues. With a little planning and making some key team decisions, many of these major tax hazards can be avoided.

THE HARD WORK IS WORTH IT

Being a business owner is certainly a lot of hard work, but it is also totally worth it. And it's not necessarily true that business owners have to pay a lot of taxes when starting out. If we plan correctly then we can actually make out pretty profitably and get away from some of those taxes. So, I encourage you to practice magic wand thinking. Get totally clear on what you need and want from life, and begin making a game plan for how to make those things the same. Set small goals first and go from there. With proper planning and a supportive family, success can be within your reach.

About Brett

Brett S. Parker is passionate about educating people on the skills needed to reach their personal and financial dreams. He is a certified business success coach, and is focused on helping people achieve their goals and ambitions, and increase their belief in themselves. Whether it's coaching clients on starting their own small business or giving a keynote presentation, Brett uses his knowledge, experience and passion to educate and inspire others.

As a business owner, Brett understands the struggles and challenges that entrepreneurs and those interested in starting their own businesses face. Before becoming a full-time business and success coach, Brett started Parker Tax Service to not only maximize the tax returns of his clients, but to also make finances more manageable. Leveraging all of the skills that he has acquired, including his bachelor's degree in Accounting, Brett has been able to help thousands of clients deal with finances in a more professional manner.

Married with children, Brett tries to give back to the community by volunteering for causes that he wholeheartedly supports. As a strong advocate for the freedom of humanity, Brett has made it his personal commitment to give time and money to combat human trafficking. In his free time, Brett enjoys spending time with his family, playing and watching sports, reading, and learning new things. Brett also volunteers as a football coach for children to help them pursue their dreams.

Brett Parker is a member of the National Society of Tax Professionals and the National Association of Tax Professionals.

You can connect with Brett at:
- info@lesstax123.com
- www.lesstax123.com

CHAPTER 8

THREE SECRETS FOR BUSINESS SUCCESS

BY ANDY WILKS, CPA, MBA

This book is titled *KEEP IT!* I interpret that to mean that you "EARN IT" (Profit) first and then organize your operation to keep what you earned. Many business owners never intentionally get to the "KEEP IT" stage.

Years ago, I had a client that taught me a lot about what a successful business must have, because he didn't have much of it, but through hard work he had a measure of success anyway. The issue was that he never achieved his full potential because of the things that he didn't do. You can achieve a level of success in the way you run your business, but never reach the full potential of what you could achieve for yourself and your family by applying the success secrets.

My client was an electrical contractor. He started as a one-man operation and as he gained some success he began to hire journeymen and licensed electricians to expand his business. He was committed to providing good, professional service to his customers.

When I came onto the scene, he had 17 trucks with electricians

79

doing a brisk business. His business consisted of new construction for a large home builder and repair work for individuals. I spent some time in his office and discovered that when a service call customer contacted his office, the work order was created, but it was laid on the stack to be scheduled.

The immediate issue I observed was there was no 'follow through' to assigning and scheduling the service work order. Later a customer would call to ask when the serviceman was scheduled, which would cause a scrabble in the office to find the work order in the stack, to determine who was assigned to complete the work. This caused frustration for the customer.

The other obvious aspect of the business that was a problem was when an electrician on a service repair order would go to the customer's location and diagnose the problem, then he would have to leave the location to get parts to complete the repair. Many of the repairs required the same parts, but these parts were not stocked on the trucks. This resulted in non-productive time for the electrician.

I helped this business owner implement some basic systems that would allow tracking of the scheduled work orders, so that information about who was to do the work and when it was scheduled to be completed was easily available to the office staff when a customer called. It also provided the electrician with a clear expectation of when the work should be completed.

We also developed a standard load list for the service trucks, based on the most common jobs, that provided the electricians with the parts they needed to complete their work orders. This eliminated some of the non-productive "parts chasing."

The business owner was an intelligent person using QuickBooks for his accounting to keep track of deposits and checks written. When we talked about how his business was doing, he had no idea. There was no information coming out of his system to give him feedback. Basically, if he had money in the bank, he was doing good. He had no way to know how productive his employees were, or which were the most profitable jobs.

I also helped the business owner develop some financial controls and key indicators that would allow him to understand where he stood now, and what he could expect in the near future.

From this experience and many others during my years of working with business owners, I developed some secrets for business success. I want my clients to reach their full potential with their business and not have stunted growth – as the electrical contractor experienced. I work with my clients to encourage them to implement success secrets in their businesses to achieve their full potential. I am focusing on three of the most important secrets.

<u>SUCCESS SECRETS</u>

1. **Clear vision for the company**
2. **Leadership**
3. **Marketing Systems**

1. Vision

Historically, 85% of new small businesses will not survive five years. A significant factor in this large number of failures is a lack of vision. The business owners did not spend enough time at the beginning identifying the critical elements for the business to be successful long term.

Having a successful business requires developing a vision for the business – to know what success for it will look like. You cannot expect that just because you open your doors and have a great product that you will be successful. Over the years, I have seen several new business owners start out with dollar signs in their eyes and be out of business six months later.

In broad strokes, the owner(s) must be able to decide what the business will provide to their customer and understand why their customer would buy from them. This must be followed up with how the money flows to make it profitable. After the broad strokes, it is time for the detail strokes to refine the vision. An owner must give thought to the future growth of the business to ensure the business will have the capacity to meet the owner goals and desired income.

Let's use the example of a barber shop. In this business model, the person doing the work is physically limited by the number of customers per day that they can serve. If the business owner wants to make more money than what they can personally do, they will have to add additional capacity by adding another barber or opening another shop. This is a decision the business owner needs to assess, because maybe they should pick a different business model.

Be clear in understanding how the business will make a profit, because without profit, it will end up in the 85% failure group. A successful owner is required to accurately think through the process of how the profit gets made. This will define the resources and processes needed to produce the profit.

2. Leadership

Running a business can be described like riding a bicycle. You need to know where you are headed, understand the tool you are using to get there, and measure if you are on track to get there. You need resources, adequate energy and balance, and you must watch for obstacles and outside issues trying to knock you off track.

When I was in the Army, we used a 5-paragraph operations order. Using it made sure everyone in the unit knew our mission, resources, and how we were planning to accomplish it. It is also essential in business that everyone in your

THREE SECRETS FOR BUSINESS SUCCESS

business knows what you are trying to accomplish and how you are trying to do it.

A business needs clearly-defined goals. Goals need to be established for long term and short term. You should establish a 5-year goal that clearly defines what your business will look like in 5 years. Then back up to 3 years to define where you would need to be in 3 years to accomplish the 5-year goal. Then come back to the 1-year goal necessary to reach the 3-year goal. Break the 1-year goal down to quarters, then months, then to weeks and finishing with what needs to be done today.

To effectively run your company, you must establish systems. Let systems run the company and people run the systems. The systems will remain and keep you going when employees leave.

Systems need a feedback loop. For example, say you establish a system for answering the phone. You train the personnel, so they know how to do it properly. But how do you know that they are actually doing it that way in the daily course of business? You need a feedback loop. Some businesses use mystery shoppers to verify performance.

The function of leaders is to keep all systems on track to achieve the goals established for the company. This requires a sub-system that produces information on what is going on in the business. This information can be in real time or after the fact.

Key Performance Indicators (KPIs) are the key indicators of progress toward a goal. KPIs bring focus to operational results that are used to verify the business is moving in the right direction to accomplish its goal. Peter Drucker, famous for developing the science of management, stated "What gets measured gets done."

An example would be measuring the number of inbound customer phone calls. If we know that 20 inbound phone calls produce 10 sales, which is the daily goal, if we are only getting 15 inbound customer phone calls, we need to act now to make the correction. This KPI provides real-time feedback. There are general categories of KPIs, but the best ones are those unique to your business.

Leaders also use trailing indicators in making decisions. These are called Key Financial Indicators (KFIs). These are trailing indicators because they come from the accounting system which is after the fact. Five basic ratios give an indication of the health of the company.

The ratios are:
1. Gross Profit Margin
2. Net Profit
3. Net Profit Margin
4. Aging of Accounts Receivable
5. Current Ratio

I grew up on a farm that was a cow-calf operation. There was always plenty of work to do. Much to the work to be done centered around the tractor. When the tractor stopped, pretty much everything else stopped because we only had one tractor. One is the loneliest number.

Don't just have one of your critical 'thing' – be it a computer, phone, generator, or manufacturing machine. Expect the unexpected. Plan for it. I do that with my computer system. I have a standby computer ready to go if something happens to the main one with constant remote data backups as well as an onsite data backup.

Another part of leadership is creating leverage. It is important to consider how to apply leverage in a positive way. As a business owner, I leverage my employees. A common example is that I should be able to expect three times the value of what I pay an employee. If I am paying someone $15 per hour, I should expect $45 per hour in production. This concept also applies in other areas of your business, such as machines, computers, and other technology. A good leader is conscious of how to use leverage in a constructive manner.

3. Marketing

Your business will fail without customers paying you money for what you do. We all know that, but I find it interesting the number of business owners who just expect the customers to show up on their own. It is not their job to find you, it is your job to reach out and bring them in.

About ten years ago, I adopted direct response marketing. It requires that you match your message to your market with the right media. Identifying your market is essential. Who is your customer? Who is your best customer? If you currently have customers, what are their common characteristics. Why do they buy from you?

In your customer base, who are the top 20% of your customers? What do they look like? A great idea is to find more customers like the top 20% because you make more money from them and they are most likely easier to serve.

Marketing is another area where you do not want to rely on any one thing that is working. You may have a Facebook ad that is killing it, but when Facebook makes a change in their system, your ad is now dead in the water.

I know of businesses that have 30 plus marketing funnels working at the same time. I have had success with direct mail, email, newsletters, Facebook ads and referrals.

Marketing is the lifeblood of your business. Dedicate time and resources to it, more customers make you more money.

Your message needs to be directed to the reason the person receiving it will be interested in your business. It needs to contain a Call-to-Action with clear instruction on exactly what you want them to do. Provide multiple ways for the customer to contact you.

These secrets of success are a starting point for having a successful business. Implementing them will help you improve your business and make more money. The more you make, you get to KEEP IT!

About Andy

Andy Wilks helps his clients build their life story by putting their business on the path to success to reach its full potential. He does this by guiding them in developing a strong action plan with specific systems.

Andy has decades of experience working with some of the largest and best-run corporations in the world including Hertz, Walgreens and Walmart. His experience at these companies laid the foundation for understanding the path to business success.

His CPA practice works principally with small businesses. His clients range from agriculture to retail and construction trades. His firm provides tax, payroll and bookkeeping services along with business consulting to his clients.

Through his years of experience, Andy developed the philosophy that building a strong business is based on delivering a memorable positive customer experience based on a foundation of well-built systems to support it. Andy believes that systems are critical for sustaining success and that you need to be intentional about what you are doing and make it happen, don't leave it to chance. Once the foundation is built, it becomes a matter of scaling the business to meet the demand.

Andy is a CPA, MBA from the University of Illinois and a retired Army Colonel. Andy has been a speaker at national conferences presenting various aspects of accounting.

Andy and his wife Joy live on an acreage, and are involved in agriculture with their horses and sheep.

You can contact Andy Wilks at:

Wilks & Co., CPA, PLLC
3909 SE 29th Street, Suite 160
Oklahoma City, OK 73115
Tel: (405) 670-3150

- Email: wilkscpa@gmail.com
- Website: www.wilkscpa.com

CHAPTER 9

WHAT DO BILL GATES, LEBRON JAMES AND BILL CLINTON ALL HAVE IN COMMON?

A STRATEGY YOU CAN USE TO MAXIMIZE YOUR TAX-DEDUCTIBLE DONATIONS

BY ALFONSO CORDERO, CPA

Give by grace what you have received by grace.

Even though I have been a trained CPA and a tax professional for over 30 years, the best way to describe what I do is to state that I provide people with solutions. I have developed an ability to help clients keep as much of their hard-earned money as possible, by minimizing their taxes.

Yes, I do offer a variety of services – from bookkeeping, tax planning, and tax preparation to problem resolution for individuals and businesses under audit. But what I really do is help people find opportunities that others can't see and relieve them of that

89

financial stress. I specialize in converting complicated situations into simple ones, by helping clients create a roadmap of small steps that they can take for solving even the most difficult tax issues.

Throughout my career, I've been involved with solving IRS cases of millions and millions of dollars in debt. My ability to investigate into other places that people just don't think about, and to prepare documentation in a way that actually makes sense, is a key strength and benefit to my clients. With an accurate representation of what is really happening, I can help clients to negotiate expenses, even if they have no proper tax documentation at all, helping them to avoid all kinds of financial trouble.

HOW A GROCERY STORE HELPED ME LEARN THE IMPORTANCE OF GIVING BACK

I like to help people. I like to see the positive results and the joy on my client's faces when I can help individuals or business owners save on their taxes. That extra money can help them grow their savings account, retirement, or fund a child or grandchild's education. Looking out for that next generation, by helping people, is what keeps me inspired with my work.

I love the saying, "Give by grace what you have received by grace." When I was nineteen years old, I was working for my father in his supermarket. Back then, people would shop for groceries and pay for them on credit. They would make a partial payment on the account to pay their balance down some, and then would charge their grocery shopping for the next week.

One day, I was working the cash register and this gentleman came in who owed $75. However, he only paid $30 to his account. Then he did his grocery shopping and charged $40 more to his account when he left. So in the end, he owed more than when he came in. When I told my dad what happened, I told him that I was confused. My dad went on to explain a very important lesson to me.

He asked me, "When you go home tonight, will you have food to eat on the table?" To which I replied, "Of course. Mom always prepares food for us." "Exactly," my dad said. He continued, "If I don't let that man take those groceries on credit, he may not have food for his family this week. And the fact that he owes me more is transitory, since next month he will get a bonus and will come back in to pay his bill in full."

Obviously, we can't always just let customers receive products or services for free, but the importance of giving grace to others and offering assistance when needed, was a deeply engraved experience that I learned that day.

MOVING TO MIAMI

While a junior in college, I had been offered an internship with the prestigious firm, Deloitte & Touche (formerly Deloitte Haskins and Sells), as well as a subsequent job after graduation. This was amazing because less than 2% of all graduating students get a job at one of the four largest accounting firms, of which Deloitte is one. While at Deloitte I worked hard and was blessed by being promoted every year, moving all the way up to senior auditor in 1983. From there, I went to work for CitiBank in the Internal Audit Department, and later, in the area of personal loans. Then in 1984, I completed my CPA exam.

But the crime rate in Puerto Rico was too much for my young family and me to handle. In fact, I was actually assaulted three times by armed robbers and held up at gunpoint! There aren't many things that will motive you like a pistol pointed at your chest. So, I told my wife and daughter that we needed to move. And with that, we relocated to Miami, Florida in 1986.

But, just six months after moving, I was out of a job. No savings, no other job opportunity, a pregnant wife and a five-year-old daughter. Yet still, I was thankful because here a businessman - an angel - gave me a job making the same amount of money as when I moved my family to Puerto Rico, for six months. This angel saw in me opportunities that I didn't see in myself at the time. So, I took the challenge and ran with it.

BE AN ANGEL FOR SOMEONE

In the fall of 1988, I stared Cordero CPA. Shortly after establishing my own business, I began giving seminars on tax and accounting services in Spanish, sponsored by the Small Business Association and the IRS. In time, I also began promoting my services through an education-based weekly radio program. Today, that program is broadcast in Miami, Kissimmee and Orlando, Florida.

When clients come to either of our two offices, during our first meeting, no matter what the problem or situation they need help with, we work with them to create a plan. And just by talking to us, you can see the expression on their faces start to change. They begin to see hope for their situation.

Clients tell me that they feel better just by coming in here. And then I'll say, "OK, this is what you need to do, and this is where you are now, and this is how we are going to move you forward. This is what we will do for you." I've learned that at the end of the day, it's all about helping people and serving clients.

So that's what I try to do. I try to be "an Angel" for people in distress because of a tax issue, or a problem with the IRS that they don't understand or know how to solve. Sure, credentials are important. But real change happens when experience and a good application of theory for real life scenarios create a positive difference for people.

MAXIMIZE YOUR DONATIONS

Maximizing charitable contributions with donations, nonprofits and private foundations, is an area that most business owners don't capitalize on. Many times, this is simply because they don't understand it and have never been exposed to these kinds of tax strategies. But with proper planning, very often setting up a private foundation or donating a highly-appraised item can dramatically offset a large tax bill.

Most people think about donations as a burden. They can feel it as a kind of obligation because somebody else asked them to give to a particular cause. Or maybe a business owner thinks about giving and donating, in terms of an amount that they give to church or charity, again mostly only when asked. People don't realize there is a broader spectrum to the topic of donation. They don't know that their charitable dollars can be maximized through proper planning and can be turned into a consistent income stream for their preferred charitable cause.

For example, did you know that the new tax code allows for a donation deduction of an item, at its fair market value, at the time of the gift? What that means is that this donation amount is not based off of a historical price or the acquisition cost, but instead on the items present value. That means that things like certain collectible items can be worth a lot more money in terms of a donation deduction.

Again, this just applies to an item, not with cash. Additionally, the "Tax Cuts and Jobs Act (TCJA) reform" allows for donation of up to 60% of an individual's income. That's a 10% increase from the former 50% allotment.

HOW A BEAT-UP CAR TURNED $10K INTO A $75K DEDUCTION

Here's a great story. I had an old client call me in November. He said, "I have a problem. My business is going so well that I'm afraid I'll going to have an enormous tax bill. Can you help me?"

We reviewed their financials, cash flow, receivables, payables, everything. And we went through a whole spectrum of questions and considered all the different kind of technicalities. But in the end, their solution was in the old 1945 collectible car they had.

This was a car he bought from a desperate seller about ten years before – for less than $2,500. My client put in another $7,500 to restore it. So, the total investment was somewhere in the $10,000 range. The good news is that the actual appraised value of the vehicle came back at over $75,000! So, yes, that's a huge $75,000 donation deduction that he can take in full or have carried forward for up to five years.

WHERE IS YOUR FORGOTTEN TREASURE?

Many of us have old collectibles or family heirlooms that are just taking up space, and other antiques that, if we're honest, aren't doing much but collecting dust. These are what I call "forgotten treasures," because they are usually stashed away in an attic, basement closet, garage, or storage space. As long as you don't have a strong emotional attachment to those items (and I suggest you probably don't if they're hidden away), then it might be worth considering donating those items if they're worth much.

In many cases, these collectible items are worth more through a tax write-off than they are valued by sentimental memories. And for business owners who are looking to minimize their tax bill, this could be a great strategy.

PRIVATE FOUNDATIONS: THE GOLDEN GOOSE OF INCOME PRODUCING TAX DEDUCTIONS

Even better than a highly-appraised collectible item, is the establishing of an income-producing entity to really maximize your charitable giving and tax deductions.

Let's say you want to help a specific charity. Maybe there's a particular cause that you are extremely passionate about. Perhaps it's helping single mothers, inner-city kids, or a food pantry. It's totally up to you. What you can do is partner with other people who share a concern for the same cause and together create a nonprofit 501(c)(3).

Maybe you own a building that you're earning rent with. If you create a nonprofit or private foundation, and gift that building to that new entity, then the income earned from that asset can be used to fund your charitable cause.

By setting up a nonprofit and donating a building that is income producing, you can actually accomplish two incredible things:
1. The donating of the property will give you a big tax savings.
2. You will create an entity that you can give to and likewise know that the income produced will be used for it's intended purposes, to support the charity or cause.

Think about it like this, many rich and famous people have created foundations in their name to support important causes that they care about. Bill Gates, Lebron James, and Bill Clinton have all done it in. Perhaps now it's your turn to benefit by benefiting others.

You can do a lot of good for your community or social cause while at the same time relieving yourself from a heavy tax load. This is one of the many benefits of our tax system. And it's worth considering if you think you may find yourself in a similar situation.

About Alfonso

Alfonso's passion is to help other people get more out of life by helping them keep more of their hard-earned money and minimize their taxes.

Alfonso believes in the power of giving back. He helps his clients do the same through maximizing their tax deductions with charitable contributions and establishing private foundations. In this way, Alfonso helps his clients to keep more of their own money, and at the same time, support the special causes they care about.

Born in Santurce, Puerto Rico, Alfonso has been living in Miami since 1986. Husband to Roxana Cordero and father of Esther and Roxana Marie, Alfonso believes in being an angel to others. With an attitude of gratitude, Alfonso lives what he teaches and in 2011 started a foundation called *Burning Flames*. His foundation serves cancer patients with meeting their financial needs and obligations.

Alfonso has been a Certified Public Accountant and a Tax Professional for over 30 years. Before starting Cordero CPA in 1988, Alfonso worked in the Internal Audit Department of Citibank Puerto Rico and at Deloitte and Touche. He is a 1980 graduate of the University of Puerto Rico with a major in Accounting.

As an experienced public speaker, Alfonso has been giving tax-related seminars on behalf of the IRS, the Small Business Association, and SCORE since 1988. His weekly radio program can be heard all across South and Central Florida, where he serves clients with two offices in the Miami and the Kissimmee / Orlando area.

Due to his well-known success in helping his clients, Alfonso is recognized as an authority on tax matters for the Hispanic community all throughout Florida.

You can connect with Alfonso at:

- Online: www.corderocpa.com
- Email: acordero@corderocpa.com
- Tel: (305) 599 - 4111